PRACTICAL YOGA

Explains the basic *asanas* (exercises) associated with
Hatha Yoga and how to perform them efficiently
and safely; how to practise relaxation and Yoga
breathing; the pros and cons of vegetarianism in a
Yoga context.

By the same author
ABOUT RICE AND LENTILS

PRACTICAL YOGA

by

HARVEY DAY

NATURE'S WAY

THORSONS PUBLISHERS LIMITED
Wellingborough, Northamptonshire

First published 1967
Second Impression 1968
Third Impression 1971
Fourth Impression 1973
Second Edition (revised and reset) 1976
Second Impression 1982

ISBN 0 7225 0351 2

Printed and bound in Great Britain by
Richard Clay (The Chaucer Press), Ltd.,
Bungay, Suffolk.

CONTENTS

FOREWORD

Yoga is not an ancient philosophy which can be adapted to modern conditions and needs. It is as modern in practice and outlook today as it was more than 25 centuries ago. It needs neither adaptation nor change.

The Yoga given here is the yoga of the Ancients; not all of it, but as much as is practicable for normal busy people who begrudge a bite of more than 10 or 15 minutes from their daily chores or pleasures.

Do as advised between these covers and you cannot help but be more healthy and contented than you are.

FALSE IDEAS ABOUT YOGA

Open any book on Yoga and read any article on the subject and you will find them illustrated with pictures of young, slim, healthy people; more often than not, attractive women. Which conveys the impression that Yoga is for the young, the supple and buoyant; that the poses illustrated are beyond the capabilities of the elderly, weak, fat and stiff-jointed. This is not so.

The impression is also given that Yoga is a system of physical exercises. This also, is incorrect.

Yoga is a Way of Life

Many Western systems of physical culture have adopted Yoga postures (not exercises) or modified them, and have done the same with Yoga breathing; but all seem to have missed its essential point. It is not a system of exercises, but a way of life; and so far none better seems to have been discovered.

Because Yoga originated in India some think it to be a form of religion – an offshoot of Hinduism – but here again, they are mistaken. Yoga has no connection with any religion. Those who practise it do not worship, accept, or recognise a deity. Anyone, of any religion, or no religion at all, can practise Yoga and gain substantial benefit. There are Roman Catholic priests and agnostics alike, who do.

Benefits Depend on You

It isn't enough to buy a book on Yoga or hang a chart

of Yoga poses on your wall. You've got to do what the book recommends and try to master the simpler postures and breathing. Not for a week or a month or until your enthusiasm wears off, but day in and day out for years, so that Yoga becomes part of your life. The benefits are enormous.

Yoga Is Threefold

Yoga is a complete philosophy because it embraces body, mind and spirit. Of these the least important is the body, which disintegrates after death and takes other forms. Mind and spirit are, however, inextricably linked with the body during your existence on this planet and events which concern one also affect the others, for they are interdependent.

Forget the Body

One aim of Yoga is to make you forget your body, because if your limbs ache and your organs give trouble your attention will be diverted to them and it will be difficult to concentrate on the development of mind and spirit. The function of the Yoga *asanas*, as the postures are called, is to make limbs and organs healthy and free them from aches and pains, and in this the breathing exercises play an important part as well.

Once your body is fit it can be kept healthy with the minimum of attention and you can progress with the development of mind and spirit.

Yoga is Not Only For the Young and Supple

Yoga is not primarily for the young and supple who can perform most of the postures with comparative ease, but for the middle-aged, the fat, and those whose bones are stiff and arthritic; whose breathing is laboured and wheezy. These are the people who benefit most from Hatha Yoga, or that branch of Yoga devoted to developing the physical body.

The mature also gain most from the practice of meditation and concentration, for the young seldom think, except about problems which concern them personally. They're too full of the joy of living to think of the problems of the world.

What Yoga Does

You will be disappointed if you expect instant results from Yoga, though you should certainly feel better from the first week or even the first day. The *asanas* will give you an easy posture and make your body lissom, which is essential as you age. Because limbs stiffen and the trunk grows rigid the elderly rick their backs and suffer slipped discs, which never seemed to have afflicted our forefathers who laboured physically hard all their lives. They bent, stretched, lifted weights and performed all sorts of manual labour. If they suffered, it was from the effects of an unbalanced diet, lack of vitamins, poverty, malnutrition and evil housing.

Yoga breathing will improve anyone, no matter how fit, both physically and mentally and spiritually. For the sedentary worker it is invaluable. It will clear a mind clogged by sitting all day at a desk in one position, in a heated atmosphere, doing dreary routine tasks. It oxygenates the blood as no other type of breathing can; and it helps in meditation and concentration.

Asanas and Yoga breathing induce a tremendous sense of well being and a spiritual uplift that makes for contentment. They help one to relax completely and in this day and age there is a greater need for relaxation than anything. People are finding it more difficult to relax than in any period of our civilization, so before going any further, I shall deal with the problem of *Stress*.

Stress

Almost every illness with which people *afflict themselves* is caused by *stress* of some sort. Psychiatrists sometimes called it *psychogenesis*, which, when you're paying, is much better value for money. It simply means diseases which originate in the mind: *psycho*, mind; *genesis*, in the beginning.

The Power of the Mind

Sir Heneage Ogilby, the famous surgeon, once said that a man with a contented mind will never get cancer. So, it is up to you to cultivate a contented mind, for a mind filled with *stress* may not only produce cancer but a myriad other diseases.

The first step in the search for freedom from illness should be to attend to the outer covering or carcase, where most aches and pains are felt, and try to relax, for relaxation is the exact opposite of *stress*. How is this to be accomplished?

Many Branches of Yoga

Every study has branches. This is so with Yoga, of which there are kinds, because there is not only one type of man, but many, all with different abilities and inclinations. There is Hatha, Raja, Gnana, Karma, Bhakta, Laya, Lignan-Yoni, Kundalini, Tantra and other kinds. The most common is Hatha, pronounced Ha'tha, the "a" in both syllables being long, as in far, and the accent on the first syllable. *Ha* means *sun* and *tha, moon,* and the word is symbolic, representing the union of two worlds; in this instance of Man, his Ego, with the Universe.

Hatha Yoga

Hatha Yoga teaches something that is fast being forgotten in Europe and appears to have vanished in America; the value of being calm and patient, which helps to build personal confidence. There are many benefits to be gained from practising it, for it deals with hygiene of a sort not generally practised in Britain and the *yoga asanas* or postures which ensure a proper supply of blood to all parts of the body. It strengthens the spine, the internal organs and improves the circulation. Advanced students progress to the *mudras,* a system of postures which gives control of the abdominal and other important groups of muscles, and the nervous system, which is so essential for health.

Yoga Breathing

Yoga breathing consists of *pranayama* (*prana,* breath; *yama,* cessation) or breath control, which increases fitness, gives immunity to changes of temperature and prevents disease. There is also *pratyahara* (*prati,* towards; *har,* to hold) a branch of Hatha Yoga which helps to develop patience; *dharana* (*dhar,* to hold), which develops concentration; and *dhyana* (*dhya,* to think), which assists one to meditate.

There is no need to memorise these names.

Many world-famous men have embraced Yoga and benefited from it, among them Ben-Gurion, former Prime Minister of Israel, Yehudi Menuhin, the world's finest violinist, writers, artists, and men prominent in all walks of life.

THE IMPORTANCE OF RELAXATION

Civilized living has vastly increased the number of victims suffering from degenerative diseases; that is, diseases in which the main organs or glands are affected and the condition grows progressively worse, resulting in complete deterioration and deathm Death itself is no calamity provided one has lived a healthy happy life of the normal span or more; but prolonged illness followed by death, is.

Disease and the Mind

Until recently mental and physical diseases were placed in watertight compartments, one type having no connection with the other. This has never been so in the East, where the physician's first questions to his patient are always about the state of his mind. "Are you happy? Have you any worries? What are your relations with your wife and family; with your employers?" Only when this information has been obtained, does treatment start.

Many European physicians have come round to this point of view and some, like Dr. Charles Berg the eminent psychiatrist, believe that almost all diseases have their origin in the mind, especially back troubles. "I fancy," he writes, "that a larger proportion of back troubles than any other localized symptoms, are psychogenic, in spite of the lastest fashion in slipped-disc diagnosis, unheard of in my young days."

At one period he used to waste an enormous

amount of time examining patients and subjecting them to a variety of tests to discover what was wrong. "It took experience," he says, "to 'bias' me in favour of psychogenesis. I certainly came from hospital training with my bias the other way." The mind makes a great many people prone to accidents!

His autobiography* is a revealing document. "It is not only the suicide," he writes, "whose 'mental balance is disturbed', the unconscious mind can harbour, at the same time, the antithetical impulses of destruction, self-destruction, construction and self-preservation; and express these simultaneously, in various proportions, by internal (bodily) and external activities all without the co-operation, or even the knowledge, of the conscious ego. It is from such conscious behaviour that we get, short of death or suicide, internal disturbances, called illnesses, and external disturbances called accidents."

The Complications Increase Yearly

Life grows more complicated every year. Man is subjected to ever-increasing stresses, which in turn produce new conditions and new diseases.

For instance, Floyd Williams, aged 57, who for 22 years had operated a petrol pump in an oil refinery, was told that automation was to be applied to his factory and he would be out of a job. His mind became so troubled that he woke one morning suffering from amnesia. One of his friends committed suicide. A number of workers in the factory had strokes, heart attacks and contracted stomach ulcers.

*Being Lived By My Life: Charles Berg

Peace of mind is the most precious state that Man can enjoy, but you can't have peace of mind unless you are completely relaxed, and utter relaxation of the body cannot be achieved without peace of mind. One goes hand in hand with the other. That is why it is important to learn to relax both body and mind. So let us start with the body.

Yoga teaches you to let your body go utterly limp and helps to rest your mind. A few minutes of relaxation precedes the postures and breathing and this is then followed by a period of concentration and meditation.

First Step in Relaxation

Lie on your back on the carpet. If the floor isn't carpeted, lie on a rug or a blanket folded in two. A soft firm surface gives the best rest; not one that allows your spine to sag. Place your arms parallel to your sides.

Close your eyes and allow your body to go limp. This is not as easy as it seems, especially when under stress because involuntarily the body is apt to grow tense. If your mind is troubled, thoughts will intrude and these tend to make one or more limbs taut; so think of each part of your body separately and as you do so, allow it to go limp; first feet, then legs and thighs, stomach, chest, arms, hands and finally cheeks, eyes, mouth and chin. When all this has been done you will probably find that your neck is still rigid. Make it go limp, too.

When this has been accomplished you will find that some parts have stiffened up again without you realizing it. So repeat the process and do it again and again if necessary.

When your body is completely limp, lie like that for 10 minutes and the odds are that you'll feel drowsy and fall asleep. Which may be just what you need.

As your body relaxes, try to think of nothing in particular, which is much more difficult than you imagine, as thoughts will persist in racing through your head.

After about 10 minutes – or when you wake – have a warm bath and slip into bed. Or if too drowsy, slip into bed without a warm bath. Sleep is what you need and deep sleep is the finest form of relaxation known. If you get that you will have accomplished the first step in Yoga.

The Need for Rest

Most people don't realize how essential is the need for complete rest *when your body cries out for it*. Sir James Paget, the famous physician, wrote: "You will find that fatigue has a larger share in the promotion and transmission of diseases than any other single condition you can name". Many people are dying today simply from fatigue brought on by stress, physical and mental, for mental stress is the deadlier of the two.

Man is the only living creature who will not rest when really tired. Often because of financial or other reasons he keeps going when well past the point of physical exhaustion, and in middle age and after this can be really dangerous.

Sleep Alkalinizes the Body

Sound sleep and complete relaxation alkalinize the body as no medicine can. In fact, medicines don't.

Today people fly to doctors because they can't

sleep and doctors (some of whom can't sleep, either) who are powerless in the face of present-day conditions, prescribe drugs. One woman who died recently from an overdose of drugs, had been given a year's supply by her doctor!

A top executive under extreme pressure may be told: "Take it easy. Go off to the Canaries for three months and lie in the sun". But, who is going to do his work, which piles up; and if he can be dispensed with for three months, why not for six – a year – or for ever?

"Every household," said William Lyon Phelps, when he was President of Yale, "should contain a cat, not only for decorative and domestic values, but because the cat in quiescence is medicinal to irritable, tense men and women.

"In spite of all the physicians and hospitals and books that endeavour to induce them to relax, few human beings understand the art of repose. Now when a cat decides to rest, he not only lies down; he pours his body on to the floor like water. It is reposeful merely to watch him."

When our puss rises from sleep his first act is to stretch; front legs, then back legs. He bends his back, arches it into a hump, shakes the sleep violently from his eyes and makes for the door.

Stretch When You Wake

Yogis advocate complete stretching of the limps and back on waking. This, practised every morning, tends to keep the body supple. Most people crawl from bed with stiff limbs and sleep still in their eyes, totter in a half-drugged state to the bathroom, splash a little warm water over their eyes, bundle into their clothes and rush off to work. Then they sit cramped over desks or in cars, or stand about all day in factories. No wonder they feel stiff and stale.

YOGA ASANAS

Even today hundreds of millions of Asians and Africans don't sit on chairs or eat at tables. They sit cross-legged or squat on their haunches on flat feet, positions most Europeans find it impossible to maintain for more than a few seconds without suffering agony.

These positions, however, come naturally to them. Sitting cross-legged is the easiest and most restful way of sitting. The yogis call it the Easy Pose but it is nothing of the sort to people accustomed to sitting on chairs. If you wish to practise Yoga you should try to sit in this attitude for a few minutes every day till it becomes natural.

Those who try it say at first that they'll never get used to it. But most of them said the same thing when fitted with dentures. "I'll never be able to talk and eat with this lot in my mouth!" Within weeks they forget all about them.

If desks were low and had long broad seats so that people could sit and type at them in the Easy Pose there would be few back aches because of faulty posture.

The Easy Pose
This is illustrated in Fig. A1. Sit as shown, on a thick carpet or rug, with crossed legs, hands gently resting on the knees. At first your knees will stick up in the air and the position will be anything but easy. Practise for a *few seconds* every day and press the

knees down *gently* till in time the hip joints become flexible. Don't use force otherwise you'll stretch ligaments that have been shortened by years of sitting on chairs. The elderly may take weeks or even months to accustom themselves to this position, but it's worth persevering.

Siddhasana

When you have mastered the Easy Pose you should attempt *Siddhasana* or the Perfect Pose. Sit on the carpet and stretch both legs out in front. Bend the left leg at the knee and place the heel under the perinium, as shown in Fig. A2. Then fold the right leg across till the heel touches the pubic bone. Place the hands on the knees, palms outwards, the last three fingers stretched out easily, the first finger bent so that it lies under the thumb. Though this is a more difficult pose, don't be discouraged. Practise daily till your joints grow supple and remember each time you unwind with groans that nothing worth doing is easy.

Until you've mastered *Siddhasana*, meditate in the Easy Pose. If you can't do even the Easy Pose, sit upright in a straight-back chair.

The ideal position for meditation is the *Lotus Seat* or *Padmasana* but as this is a book mainly for beginners, there is no point in describing it. The Perfect Pose gives your body a fixed base on which to balance effortlessly and naturally. If, however, you wish to graduate to an advanced state of Yoga you must master the Lotus Pose, for there are certain postures known as *mudras* which cannot be accomplished without it.

Hatha Yoga, the type dealt with here, is meant to make you fitter and your joints supple. According

A1

A2

to Dr. Vansant Rele, a medical man who has made a close study of the subject, Yoga postures increase the flow of blood to the brain, help you to concentrate and meditate and make your glands, on which health largely depends, function efficiently.

There will be many whose joints are so stiff and bodies so racked with pain that they cannot even think of attempting the Easy Pose. For them the upright sitting position in a chair is better than none. The breathing exercises alone will bring much benefit.

Yoga should be started at as early an age as possible, when limbs are supple, so that poses become second nature.

The aim of Yoga is physical, mental and spiritual well-being. It will be difficult to apply yourself mentally if the body proves troublesome.

The purpose of most Western systems of physical culture is to increase the bulk of the muscles and make them bigger, rounder and more powerful, and in the process to increase the circulation of the blood. These systems must not be condemned for they serve a purpose, though a limited one.

Asanas

The purpose of Yoga *asanas* or postures is very different. They send a rich supply of blood to the brain and the spinal cord. They twist the spinal cord and massage it gently. They stretch the spine and *warm* the body. Some asanas are extremely difficult and cannot be performed except by long and arduous practice. But all Yoga postures bring benefit, even the simplest and easiest, and if practised regularly will make an enormous difference to health.

Shri Aurobindo Ghose

Shri Aurobindo Ghose came to England at the age
of seven, entered Manchester Grammar School and
went on to King's College, Cambridge. He turned
in brilliant papers for the Indian Civil Service but
failed to get in – because he could not ride!

On his return to Calcutta he took a position with
Maharaja Sayaji Rao Gaekwad of Baroda, but
could find no peace. The job was too worldly so he
left to become Editor of *Yugantar* and of *Karma Yogin*
and inspired a school for Indian independence. He
was arrested during the Alipur Bomb Case, thrown
in jail and eventually released. In jail his
transformation of *sadhana* took place, an event
commemorated by the Government of Bengal, who
placed a tablet there.

Founded an Ashram

Aurobindo, as he was always known, found refuge
in Pondicherry, a French settlement in South India
and founded an *ashram* which became world famous
and visited by pilgrims from all over India, Europe
and America. Here he became a great "religious"
teacher, for he was equally acquainted with
Plotinus, St. Thomas Aquinas, the Greek
philosophers, the Upanishads, Sankara, the
teachings of the Gita, and other religious and
philosophical works. Towards the end of his life he
took a vow of silence.

Because he had practised Yoga since childhood
he never suffered a day's illness and when he died in
1950 at the age of 78 he still looked young, without
a wrinkle or crease on his face. The Chief Medical
Officer of French India held up the funeral because
after two days in a tropical climate his body showed

no sign of decomposition, though this usually sets in within 12 hours. The Medical Officer also recorded that Aurobindo's body was "covered with a supernatural light". Could this have been his astral body hovering over the earthly carcase?

The yogis believe that each human is allotted a certain span of life and if you live as you should, your body will be in perfect condition when you die. Death will come when the electrical charge which keeps you going has run out. With them, death is not final and there are other states in which one develops. Some call this reincarnation and though there is circumstantial evidence, there is no actual proof of an after-life.

This doesn't really matter. What matters is that as long as you live on this planet your body and mind should be healthy and your spirit buoyant, so that you can fully enjoy your life and make it as creative as possible.

Rhythmic Exercises

In Yoga there are no fits and starts, no jerks, no straining of tendons and muscles. Yogic postures regulate the action of heart, lungs, brain, liver, kidneys, the glands and sex organs and, by doing them regularly, you can ward off degenerative diseases such as diabetes, rheumatism and arthritis.

In orthodox systems the superficial muscles are exercised and increased in bulk; in Yoga the organs and glands are toned up. The strengthening of these results in freedom from disease, which is what most people desire. A little patience is needed. Yoga *asanas* may be done in any order but a good one to start with is *paschimottasana* because it warms one and if done properly even induces perspiration.

According to the ancient lore the breath flows through the *Brahma Nadi* or *Shushumna* and rouses the gastric fire. This may or may not be the case, but it is an excellent abdominal exercise, stimulates kidney, liver and pancreas and helps to prevent piles and diabetes. The posterior muscles and the muscles at the backs of the thighs – the hamstring muscles known as semi-tendonosis, biceps and semi-membranosus – are fully stretched. Do this exercise regularly and you will never pull a muscle while bending, no matter how old you may be. The spine grows elastic and the epigastric nerves, bladder, the prostate gland and the lumbar region are all kept healthy.

If these seem somewhat exaggerated claims, do the exercise regularly for six months and await results.

Paschimottasana

Lie flat on your back; then stiffen your body and rise gradually into a sitting position.

Now exhale and bend forward. Grasp your toes and bend as far down as you can go. Beginners, unless young and supple, are seldom able to place the head on the knees or on the carpet. But if you do this regularly you should soon be able to do so. Impossible? Keep on trying.

Retain this position for five seconds, then raise your body to a sitting position and exhale while doing so. Repeat five times. There is no need to increase the number of repetitions, for increasing them only adds to the monotony of exercising. Each day, however, try to pull your body and head further down till first the knees and then the floor is reached. When you get to this stage try to keep your

knees locked with your calves touching the carpet.
The effect will be felt on the backs of the thighs,
behind the knees and in the lumbar region, parts of
the body which get little exercise once one leaves off
playing games.

Surya Namaskar

A fine exercise can be taken from the *Surya
Namaskars*. Some years ago Shrimant Balasahib
Pandit Pratinidhi, the Rajah of Aundh, wrote a
little book called *The Ten Point Way to Health* in
which he maintained that one of the *Surya Namaskars*
(literally Sun Prayers) cured him of constipation (a
family complaint!) and stated that Yoga breathing
would prevent and *cure* tuberculosis. He was a
remarkably fit man – but no such claim is made
here.

Stand erect, heels together and your body
upright but not stiff. Inhale deeply, raise your arms
above your head and bend back as far as possible
without overbalancing. Spine and rib box will be
stretched and expanded by this.

Exhale, using the stomach muscles to push out
the air and while doing so, bend forward and place
the palms of your hands on the carpet a few inches
in front of your toes. If this can't be managed, get
down as far as you can; with practice you'll get
lower and lower. Keep your knees locked, and while
doing so, press your chin into your neck in what is
known as a chin lock. This, says Dr. Rele, has a
beneficial effect on the thyroid gland.

If stiff the strain will be felt in the small of your
back as you bend forward and lean back. The real
strength of the body lies not in the arms but in the
small of the back, stomach, and thighs. The

movements of this *Namaskar* relieve pelvic congestion and constipation.

Note the three points: rigid legs, complete exhalation using stomach muscles; chin lock.

Now inhale and step back with the left foot. Bend the right leg but retain the chin lock. Exhale and move the right leg back, as in Fig. B1. Keep your knees rigid and *try* to place your heels on the floor. This will be impossible — but try. The effort stretches the thigh and calf muscles. Retain the chin lock.

Next, inhale fully, release chin lock and go down into the dip position as shown in Fig. B2. The body, from head to heels, must be on the same level. Keep rigid and exhale.

Then inhale deeply and assume the position shown in Fig. B3, your back in an inverted arch, with chest well forward. Don't bend you arms. Only the palms of your hands and your toes should be touching the floor.

Exhale and in smooth movement resume the position shown in Fig. B1. This is not as difficult as it may seem. Any effort will be felt in the arms and the small of the back. Assume the chin lock, contract the muscles of the stomach and lock your knees. This up-swinging movement strengthens the back and loosens the hip joints.

Now inhale and bring the left leg quickly forward with right knee rigid.

Finally exhale, bring the right leg up, your hands flat on the floor, your legs rigid. Try to place your head against your knees. Then rise to the original position.

Now do the exercise, moving back with the right foot. Repeat five times, using alternate feet, and

B1

B2

B3

increase one repetition each week till 10 are reached.

If you are pressed for time, do this exercise only.

Halasana or the Plough

The Plough is so called because it resembles the shape of a primitive Indian plough.

Lie flat on your back with arms stretched alongside your body, palms down. Raise your legs, keeping the knees locked (Fig. C1). Then tilt your legs over slightly and place your hands against the small of your back, supporting it (Fig. C2). Continue the tilting movement till your legs go right over your head and your toes touch the carpet behind you (Fig. C3). Make an effort to shove your toes as far back as you can from your head and press your chin back into your neck (Fig. C4). You will feel a gradual pull along the vertebral column and a pressure at the cervical point of the spine. This movement stretches the entire lumbo-sacral region and keeps the spine, from which the nerves radiate, healthy. It stretches your neck and places pressure on the stomach muscles, and the effect on the thyroid gland is supposed to be beneficial.

Finally, raise your legs till they are vertical, place your hands on the floor again, and lower your legs *gradually*, keeping the knees locked all the time. Repeat slowly, five times.

Sirshasana

This is the most difficult of the postures I shall describe, but with a little practice is well within the capability of almost everyone. *Sirsh* is the Sanskrit for *head*. Because of the excellent effect this has on the system it is known as the King of Asanas.

Place a cushion or folded blanket as a pad for your head. Interlock your fingers to act as a support for the head and assume the position in Fig. D1. Slowly raise the trunk of your body and your legs till they reach the position in Fig. D2. It isn't easy. If heavy or flat, or if you haven't tried it before, you will need help. Even young, active people find it difficult at first. Move the furniture away so that if you fall you won't hurt yourself.

After a few tries most people lie back and gasp, "I'll never do this!" Once you get into this position, (Fig. D3), the rest is easy. Continue raising your legs till they are vertical. Your head and elbows give you a triangular base. All you have to do is retain your balance. Remain inverted for five seconds, then lower your legs to the position in Fig. D2 and from there on to the floor. Don't let yourself go limp suddenly or you'll fall with a clang.

Is the effort worth while? Yes. Once mastered, *Sirshasana* is easy. A flow of blood is sent to the brain, which tones the sympathetic nervous system and relieves defects of the eyes, ears, nose and throat. Venous blood, which normally has to rise against the force of gravity, is now assisted by gravity. Medical men say that *Sirshasana* has a beneficial effect on the pituitary and pineal glands and the gonads and is of immense value to dyspeptics and neuresthenics.

Some of the claims for it border on the fantastic: that it helps to cure diseases of the liver, spleen, lungs and genito-urinary system, renal colic, deafness, diabetes, piles, pyorrhea, constipation and digestion; but there is little doubt that sufferers from these diseases gain relief from practising *Sirshasana*. An Indian medical man told me that

D1

D2

D3

uterian and ovarian diseases are relieved by this posture; also, that in males sterility tends to disappear, but no such claims are made here.

Bhujangasana

Bhujang is Sanskrit for *cobra* and in this posture the head and trunk are raised like that of a cobra raising itself to strike.

Lie face down with the arms bent, the palms flat on the floor and in line with the shoulders.

By pressing firmly on the palms, raise the head and chest, gradually but forcibly. Don't jerk. Bend the spine, raising it little by little, so that you can feel the effect on each vertebrae as the pressure travels from the cervical, dorsal and lumbar to the sacral regions. The body, from thighs to toes should be touching the floor, with a gap under the legs and ankles, of course. The arms will be partly bent. Exert as much pressure as you can, till the effect is felt in the sacrum at the base of the spine.

This exercise bends the spine in the opposite way to that in the Plough and helps to keep the spine supple and elastic. Pains in the back are relieved and the abdominal muscles stretched. It is good for the viscera and helps to relieve constipation.

Now relax and lie prone once more. Do this six times slowly but forcibly. Don't hurry and don't jerk.

Dhanurasana

This is an extension of *bhujangasana* and more difficult. It need not be attempted until your spine has become flexible by doing the *cobra* pose. *Dhanur* means *bow* and in this the arms and legs resemble the strings of a bow while the trunk and thighs represent the wooden portion.

Lie face down. Fold the legs back over the thighs. Grasp the right ankle with the right hand and the left ankle with the left hand and raise your body by pulling on your ankles, so that you rest on abdomen and thighs and your spine is arched. Maintain the position for five seconds, then relax. Breathe normally.

As you pull on the ankles you will feel a distinct strain on the lower stomach muscles, the shoulder muscles and the spine. This is one exercise which helps to reduce fat on the stomach, so is specially recommended for women who want to slim. It must, however, be done in conjunction with *paschimottasana* and *halasana* because they stretch the spine and the *bow* contracts it.

Salabhasana

Salabh means *locust* and this imitates the position of the locust while eating. In photographs this seems the easiest of postures but in practice it is one of the most difficult for beginners with weak spines and stomach muscles.

Lie flat, as before, with arms parallel to the body, palms facing up. Rest your chin on the floor.

Inhale slowly and as you do so, stiffen the torso and, keeping your knees locked, raise your legs as high off the floor as you can go. The expert will succeed in raising his legs till they are vertical or almost so; but if after months of practice you can make an angle of 30 degrees with your legs and the floor, you'll be doing very well. At first inches will be all you can manage because great strength and suppleness are needed in stomach and back, and muscles most people don't realize they possess are brought into action: the serous coat consisting of translucent membrane, and three layers of involuntary unstriated fibres. One runs longitudinally from end to end; the second is circular; and the third – the innermost layer – is oblique. When these muscles grow slack, the stomach begins to protrude.

When your muscles have developed and your spine is flexible you may be able to raise your toes two or three feet off the floor without bending your knees. If you can manage a foot you'll be doing very well. This posture strengthens *all* the muscles in the abdominal region as well as the sacral, coccyxigeal and the lumbar regions and accelerates the flow of blood to them. It is the only Yoga pose which calls for a sudden and violent effort in raising the limbs. Repeat. Never do it more than three times. Try to maintain the pose for three seconds, then bring your legs down slowly, exhaling as you do so. Experts can maintain the raised position for half a minute, which may seem impossible.

Ardha-Matsyendrasana or Spine Half-Twist

Ardha means *half* and *Matsyendra* was the name of the yogi who introduced this posture into the system. It's like a rest cure after the *locust* position.

Sit upright with palms on the floor on either side, the left leg out in front with the knee locked, the right leg bent so that the sole of the foot is parallel with, and touching the right thigh (Fig. E1). *(see overleaf)*

Raise the left leg and place it a little in front of, and to the right of the right knee. At the same time press the heel of the right leg hard against and slightly under the left thigh, and place the right arm

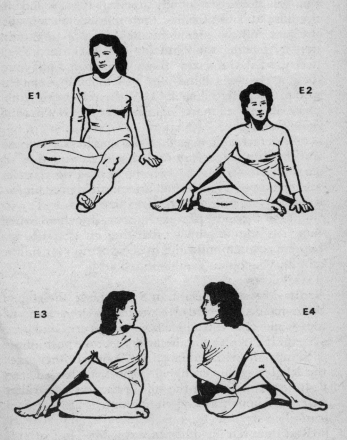

along the left leg (Fig. E2).

Then twist the body, face to the left and tuck your left arm into the bend of the waist as shown in Fig. E3. It sounds complicated but is easy. Retain the pose for five seconds; then release yourself and perform the movement in the opposite direction; that is, placing the right leg out, tucking the left heel under the right thigh, twisting right and tucking the right hand round the back into the left side of the waist (Fig. E4). When you do the final part of the exercise, use a smooth, swivelling movement.

In previous exercises the spine has been stretched back and forward; contracted and expanded. This gives it a lateral twist, gently massaging muscles and organs and has been found of immense value in lumbago and muscular rheumatism.

It also helps to prevent slipped discs and when done in conjunction with the other postures, prevents constipation and dyspepsia.

Trikonasan

Trikona means *triangle*, and this is a position of triangles. Stand erect with the feet between two and three feet apart. Stretch your arms out on either side, parallel with the shoulders, palms down. Bend slowly to the left, keeping arms rigid, till the tips of the fingers of the left hand touch the toes of the left foot. Maintain the position for five seconds, then rise. Now bend to the right and touch the toes of the right foot with the fingers of the right hand. The left arm will be extended horizontally, in a line with the body. Do this three times in each direction. This stretches and squeezes the intercostal muscles alternately and is of especial value to anyone who has suffered a fracture of the hip or thigh-bone, which renders one leg shorter than the other. The spine is also stretched in a new direction. Keep knees locked throughout the exercise.

As this is an elementary but practical treatise, I shall dwell only on two more exercises, both for the stomach. Max Sick, the famous Austrian strong man, who introduced muscle control, learnt these exercises from the yogis.

Uddiyana Bandha

Stand with your legs apart and exhale, using the stomach muscles to drive out every particle of air. Bend slightly and place your hands on your thighs to give greater effect to the effort. Then press on the thighs and raise your chest – but don't inhale. As there is no air in the lungs a vacuum is created which draws in your stomach so that it seems to press against your spine. Relax and breathe in. Repeat this five times, each time using all the force you can to empty your lungs. This is excellent for relieving constipation, for it assists peristalsis.

Nauli Kriya

This . is an extension of *Uddiyana Bandha* and stimulates the viscera and the entire alimentary system.

Stand with your legs apart and hands on the thighs, as before. Bend forward and expel the air from your lungs as you did for *uddiyana bandha*. Contract your stomach and draw the stomach muscles back. Then try to force the muscles of the stomach out. If you succeed they will jut forward in a thick, ropelike formation. They will appear in the centre, leaving a gulf on either side. This is known as *Madhyama Nauli*. Layers of fat on the stomach will prevent you doing this; but once you succeed you can force the "rope" of muscle to the left side of your stomach, and to the right, a churning movement, which is a sure cure for constipation and will relieve all gastro-intestinal disorders. It tones the liver and pancreas and makes hepatitis and diabetes unlikely.

Orthodox exercises for developing the stomach muscles contract and expand them, usually under resistance and, if persisted in develop large, powerful muscles which become taut and stiff. *Nauli* makes them as supple as elastic.

You Need Strong Stomach Muscles

Strong, flexible stomach muscles are even more necessary for the middle-aged than the young. In youth muscles are naturally pliable from running and games and have not deteriorated or accumulated fat. On reaching middle age, however, men think they can still perform the feats they used to when young, and attempt lifting excessively heavy loads, which throws a strain on the stomach. They move pieces of heavy furniture in sudden jerks, with knees locked and back bent, instead of with straight back and bent knees – and rupture themselves.

Recently a powerfully built friend of mine tried to lift a heavy load of compost at the end of a fork; because he hadn't braced himself correctly and his stomach muscles were much too slack, he ruptured himself. Hernia is a condition all too common among middle-aged men who have let themselves run to seed.

If only they practised the *bandha* and the *nauli two* or *three* times every day, they would have an insurance against hernia. These movements would take them no more than a *few seconds* once they were mastered. This, though seeming incredible, is true, for health flows from a strong flexible stomach and spine.

YOGA BREATHING

The purpose of Yoga breathing is twofold: to maintain your body in a state of perfect health, and help you to attain *samadhi* or release of the spirit. To achieve this you must observe certain restraints (*yamas*) and observances (*niyamas*) and practise *asanas* and *pranayama*. You need not use these terms and can refer to them as *exercises* and *breathing*.

To get the utmost benefit from Yoga you must do the exercises and the breathing; for then you get physical and mental control. It is the only system which has, worked into it, breathing which purifies the blood, tones the nervous system and the glands, and helps you to *think clearly*.

Reading this book won't be the slightest use unless you put the instructions into play and carry them out daily. So, don't at first attempt too much. The lives of most people are so full that in time a system of exercises, or breathing, taken up with immense enthusiasm, is bound to pall unless you can see and feel how good it is.

A complete Yoga course cannot be mastered without years of application, so let your aims be modest and make Yoga a habit.

Chest Development
All orthodox systems of breathing aim at developing a wide, deep chest. Yoga doesn't. Though your chest will inevitably grow deeper, the aim of Yoga breathing is to enable you to use the

maximum amount of oxygen drawn in with the air, and then expel the maximum amount of waste products.

When you eat and food is digested and passes into the bloodstream in microscopic quantities, at least nine chemical changes take place before it can be used by the organs. When a molecule of nutriment enters the blood it meets a tiny particle of oxygen, which produces energy by means of combustion. Waste in the form of CO_2 (carbon dioxide) is thrown off, carried along the venous system and expelled through the lungs into the atmosphere.

By some means, though we don't know quite how, Yoga breathing enables more oxygen to pass into the blood at each inhalation than any other form of "deep" breathing. Because it does this those who practise Yoga feel less tired than those who do not, and rarely suffer from exhaustion. They also recuperate more rapidly.

Ether, Odic Force, Bio-Cosmic Energy

The amount of air you breathe depends not on the size of your chest but on the strength and flexibility of your diaphragm. The yogis were the first to realize how this powerful muscle acts. In Yoga breathing air is drawn into both the lower and upper portions of the chest and then by using the diaphragm and the stomach muscles, is almost completely expelled. In this way (1) the heart is strengthened, (2) blood circulation in liver and spleen improved, (3) peristalsis of the stomach and intestines increased and, (4) constipation cured.

The nerves are strengthened and toned up in a way that baffles medical science, for there is still much that doctors and scientists don't know. The wonder of it is that the yogis knew anything about it more than 2,500 years ago. They say that *prana* or life force is drawn into the blood and flows along the nerves, strengthening them. Dr. M. Bircher-Benner called this Chemical Energy; labelled it Ether, Bio-Cosmic Energy and Cosmic Orgone Energy.

Electrical Life Force

Call it what you will, this is probably the electrical energy which emanates from the brain and flows along the nerves, translating thoughts into actions and enabling us to think, learn and remember. When this electrical force falters we grow ill; when it fails and becomes extinct, we die. How it is nurtured and increased in strength, we don't know. It starts to fail late in middle life – sometimes in early middle life – when the bounce goes out of a man's step, his reactions becomes slower, and he no longer enjoys running. A fortunate few maintain fitness and virility till well past middle life, but almost anyone can maintain and even increase this *prana* by practising Yoga breathing and performing some of the advanced Yoga exercises.

The Aura

It has been the habit of scientists and other materialists to scoff when spiritualists, clairvoyants and other sensitives said they could see the human *aura* (from the Greek *air*), a coloured translucent edging which envelopes the body, but in January 1967 Professor Pavel Gulyayev, head of the laboratory of physiological cybernetics at Leningrad University, and his associates, discovered that animal and human nerves, muscles and hearts create an electrical field in the air and an electro-auragram was obtained and recorded during a meeting of the Leningrad Society of Natural Sciences.

The instrument recorded the existence of an electrical field around a nerve of a frog at 25 centimetres, and round a human heart at a distance of 10 centimetres. And this applies equally to nerves, muscle, heart and brain. The experiments showed that the human body has an electrical field around it, the strength of which can be recorded with a highly sensitive probe-amplifier. Professor Gulyayev says: "Electro-auragramming changes radically our views on living organisms, shedding light on the mechanism of biological relationships between them, relationships which were impossible to prove materially before". How then, did the yogis know so very long ago?

William James – Psychologist

William James, brother of Henry James the writer, had a friend who practised Yoga breathing and exercises and wrote that he "seemed to have succeeded in waking up deeper and deeper levels of will and intellectual power in himself, and to have escaped from a decidedly menacing brain-condition of the 'circular' type, from which he had suffered for years. ... A profound modification has unquestionably occurred in the running of his mental machinery".

While K.T. Behanan was at Yale University he wrote a thesis on Yoga for his Doctorate of Philosophy and, naturally, practised both breathing and *asanas*. He commented: "In the years before taking up these practices I was in a generally run-down condition which may be colloquially described as one of lack of 'pep'. Needless to say I did not commence yogic postures for any amelioration of these ills; on the contrary, the mere belief that an objective study would be facilitated by practising the exercises myself, led me to undertake them.

"A few months after the beginning of the practices in April 1932, a distinct change was noticeable in my health. No work, physical or mental, could tire me so rapidly as it did before. This phase may be summarised as an increase in my resistance capacity or power of endurance. My susceptibility to frequent headaches also was diminished considerably".

Nervous Centres

Within the past century scientists have maintained that there are four main nervous centres in the body: cerebrum, cerebellum, medulla oblongata, and solar plexus, which act as rectifiers and distributors of life force and that the pineal and pituitary glands are sensitive inductors.

But more than 25 centuries ago yogis said that there were centres of life force within the body, called *chakras*. There are twin centres in the spinal column called *pingala* (masculine) and *Ida* (feminine), between which runs *shushumna* like a tube. At the end of this lies *kundalini* or the potential divine energy.

Shushumna they said, was the central trunk of the Tree of Life and at points along it are the six *chakras* or nervous centres. At the base is the *Muladhara Chakra*, and those who can control this centre will remain free from disease.

Next is the *Svadisthana Chakra*, which rises from the sacral plexus, and control of this makes one greatly beloved.

What we call the solar plexus is the *Manipura Chakra*, control of which makes one a Master of healing.

The *Anhata Chakra* lies in the heart, and we know now from researches carried out by Dr. Allan J. Brady and a team of scientists at the Los Angeles County Heart Association, that the heart has muscle cells which act as miniature electric batteries. Those who control this *chakra* can exert psychic power.

The *Vishudda Chakra* is situated below the larynx and is connected to the pharyngeal plexus. Those who control it retain vigour far beyond the normal span.

The *Anja Chakra* lies between the eyebrows, in the pineal gland, and gives outstanding occult power.

There is another, the *Shasrara Chakra*, but this lies outside the actual body and in illustrations is shown above the head as a sort of powerful aura. Control over this will enable one to prolong life and energy indefinitely.

These are the main nervous centres. There are also minor centres.

At the turn of the century when the West started to learn about Yoga, these theories were ridiculed, but now we believe many of them because we have advanced along the path of science and some of our findings coincide with theirs. Professor Joseph Needham, F.R.S., said during a series of lectures on the Third Programme of the B.B.C., that the ancients in India possessed the secret of atomic power! Did they realize the futility of possessing it —

or did it destroy their civilization, as perhaps Atlantis was destroyed?

Many mysteries remain unsolved about races and civilizations in the past: the Incas, the Aztecs, the people who inhabited the Gobi desert and built magnificent cities which now lie deep under the sand. How much did they know? Did they misuse their power as we are now misusing ours, and is that why they were obliterated and the knowledge they accumulated, lost?

Perhaps we will learn from them and mend our ways before it is too late – or does one never learn anything from history?

The Aim of Yoga Breathing

The aim of Yoga breathing is not chest development though that should automatically follow; it is *samadhi* or release of the spirit. It gives control over the vagus nerve (Latin: *vagus*, wandering) which sends branches to the larynx, pharynx, heart, lungs, stomach and intestines and helps to regulate the action of these organs. It is the tenth cranial nerve and supplies most of the internal organs.

Control of the vagus nerve gives mastery over, but not suppression of, the emotions. Fear and worry affect the heart and the stomach, increase the rate of blood circulation and cause the glands to secrete hormones in the blood – some good, some harmful, depending on the emotions aroused. Being able to control (not suppress) the emotions is a valuable aid to health and happiness.

A Rediscovered Function

Dr. Bernard Aschner says: "The heart specialist

pays special attention to the diaphragm. This is a very important item, for when this organ of respiration, which is shaped like a slingshot, is displaced too far upwards, it may press against and restrict the heart. ... It marks a great step forward that modern medicine has *rediscovered* the relationship between heart and stomach, which has as its intermediary the vagus nerve, common to both organs".

Aschner was right when he used the word "rediscovered", for the yogis knew what the functions of this nerve were.

Vagus Nerve
The vagus has two sets of fibres: those that convey impulses inwards, and others that convey them outwards. The first induces inspiration and stops expiration; when the second set is stimulated the opposite process takes place. These fibres are brought into operation and stimulated by the expansion and contraction of the air vesicles of the lungs, at the end of the vagus nerve.

Your Aura
According to the yogis every human is surrounded by an aura or subtle emanation from the body, which cannot be seen by the human eye unless the seer is highly psychic. Fear, hatred, jealousy, happiness, goodwill and other emotions produce auras of different colours and different odours. If for instance, you have an inherent fear of dogs, they will smell or see your aura, bristle and show their teeth, because fear breeds fear. They think you're afraid because you intend to harm them, and take defensive action. Without this fear which is

implanted in him, man would walk unarmed and unharmed in a jungle filled with wild animals, as the yogis do. If emotions are controlled, the colour and odour of the aura will change.

Yogis say that breath (oxygen) travels not only into the circulation but along the nerves. This has so far not been proved though science may one day do so. They also maintain that Yoga poses and breathing will help to prolong life to a great age. Our aim is limited to giving you health of body and peace of mind.

Breathing the Yoga Way

Start to inhale slowly so that the lower portion of the lungs starts to fill. Then gradually swell the rib box with air. First, do this in stages, then combine the operations in one smooth inhalation. With practice this will become easy and natural.

When you've inhaled fully, reverse the process. Empty the upper chest first, then the rib box, and finally by stiffening the stomach muscles, expel the air completely from your lungs. No matter how hard you try, some air will remain, but this doesn't matter.

Yoga breathing makes the rib box flexible, exercises the small muscles between the ribs and makes them supple. These are the intercostal muscles. As one grows older and takes less exercise these become covered with fat and lose their elasticity. Fat men and women lose the use of their intercostals and breathe almost entirely from the lower ribs and stomach, and as a result tend to open their mouths when breathing. They don't breathe. They puff. Full inhalation gives them "stitch", and fat stomachs prevent complete inhalation. None of these in itself is deadly, but cumulatively they tend to breed disease.

Practise this method of breathing in and out, fast, till you can do it easily and rhythmically, and sometimes this alone will dissipate a headache. Try it.

Position for Breathing

The ideal position for breathing is the Lotus Seat (*padmasana*) and the next best, the Perfect Pose (*siddhasana*). If you can manage neither, the Easy Pose will do. If this is irksome, sit in a straight-back chair with your back pressed against it and your feet firmly on the floor. Always sit rather than stand, though this rule is not inflexible and you can do Yoga breathing either standing or lying.

The Complete Breath

Breathe in slowly, filling the lower portion of the lungs. Suck the air into your stomach and let the lower portion of your rib box expand. Then fill the upper portion of your chest with air. Let the air go up and up and up. Don't try to *expand* your chest unnecessarily. Now hold your breath for a few seconds; then reverse the order and exhale by gradual stages; first the upper chest, then the rib box; and finally squeeze the air out by using your stomach muscles.

The three stages are known as: *puraka* (inhalation), *kumbhaka* (pause), and *techaka* (exhalation). *Kumbhaka* helps to improve stamina. In some of the breathing exercises there is no *kumbhaka*.

Kapalabhati or the Bellows

In this there is no *kumbhaka*. Sit on a soft pad or cushion with the hands resting on the knees. Breathe in, as instructed, then out, *fast* and with a full, final drive from the stomach muscles. If the time taken to breathe in is five seconds, then force the breath out in one.

Do this 10 times in succession; then rest for a few seconds. Do it 10 times again, and rest once more. Do it a third time.

Increase the number of repetitions by one each week and keep on till you can do 120 *without a pause*. There is no need to go further. This will not take as long as you imagine because when you became adept, three complete rounds (inhalation and exhalation count as one) will take no more than a second or two.

Never force the exercise or strain the lungs. If you suffer from a weak heart, do not aim at speed. Do the exercise slowly and if you feel any ill effects, stop doing it. But normal people should gain nothing but benefit.

Regular practice of *kapalabhati* will help to prevent cold, improve digestion, assist in curing constipation and should make you healthier in every way.

F.A. Hornibrook, author of that excellent book *Culture of The Abdomen* obviously based his "pumping" exercise on *kapalabhati*, but for its muscular effort and relief of constipation rather than a breathing exercise, for the intercostal group, the rectus abdominus, external and oblique, are all vigorously exercised.

The Four Bhedas
These breathing exercises are peculiar to Yoga and have not, as far as I know, been adapted to any other system.

Suryabheda
Sit in the Easy Position and try to pull your chin into the hollow of your neck above the Adam's apple. Place your left palm in front of you and fold the first and second fingers on to the palm, leaving the third and small finger free. Press the thumb gently against the side of the left nostril, blocking it, and inhale through the right nostril. Hold your breath while you shift your hand slightly to the left, freeing the left nostril and blocking the right nostril with the third and little fingers. Exhale through the left nostril.

Now inhale through the left nostril, hold your breath while you press your thumb against the left nostril and free the right. Exhale through the right. Then inhale through the right and start the whole process again.

Do this slowly, 10 times, increasing by one repetition each week till 20 are performed. This is enough. Remember – each time you exhale, use the power of the stomach muscles to expel the air; and when you inhale, take in air first through the lowest part; then the rib box, and finally the chest. Inhaling and exhaling must be smooth and rhythmic.

When done properly this exercise has a greater effect in preventing tuberculosis than any other. It also induces perspiration, raises body temperature and is excellent for all with feeble circulations.

In his book, *An Active Life*, Dr. Frederick

Barnardo, former Dean of the Medical Faculty of Calcutta, wrote that while a student at Edinburgh University, a friend introduced him to this exercise, which he did throughout his life.

"'This is the way,' said his friend, 'to keep fit and have a long life. And this is the chief exercise of the lot'.

"With that he stood in front of the window, closed one nostril, inhaled through the other, exhaled and then repeated the exercise with the other nostril. This he repeated during 10 minutes or so.

"'Gives you complete muscular control of the ribs and diaphragm,' he assured me. 'Makes you use all your lung capacity to the full, not just the top. Broadens the chest and tones up the whole system. Try it'.

"I did," writes Barnardo, "but it was some time before I was as skilled as he was. I have kept up the practice ever since, and attribute my longevity (he lived to be 95) in part to the habit of silent and controlled breathing. I know that it developed my chest, for during the three years after I started practice, my chest measurement went up to 47 inches."

Though he did not realize it, Barnardo was practising *Suryabheda*. As far as Yoga is concerned, however, chest development is not the primary aim. Their type of breathing is meant to prevent disease and provide energy.

Ujjayi
In this the breath is inhaled slowly and deeply through both nostrils with the glottis half closed so that a choking or sobbing sound is heard. When the

lungs are full, hold your breath as long as you can *without strain*; then swallow and exhale through the *mouth*. The period of holding the breath should be twice that taken to inhale. The value of this lies in *kumbhaka* for the yogic theory is that the oxygen taken into the blood by this means charges the nerves, though there is no scientific evidence of this. Let each round occupy 15 seconds and do no more than four or five.

Sitkari and Sitali

These are done to obtain a balance.

In *Sitkari* the teeth are held together till they just touch, the tongue is suspended in the middle of the mouth, and the air is sucked in between the teeth in such a way that the force of suction brings into play the muscles of the stomach. Exhale through the mouth.

Breathe in and out, forcibly, 30 times. When performed during a fast, it appeases the pangs of hunger.

In *Sitali* you breathe in through the mouth and out through the nostrils. Do this 30 times.

Both these are contrary to the teachings of Western physical culture experts but as their effects have proved beneficial, that is what really matters.

Bhastrika

This is almost the same as *Suryabheda*, except that it is rapid and rhythmic and muscular force is not used to expel the breath. Both are among the six cleansing and purifying processes known as "cleansing the nadis", which rid the body of mucus and other impurities, and are of special benefit to sufferers with bronchitis. If you have a stuffed nose *bhastrika* will clear it quickly unless the nostrils are absolutely blocked. Then only abstinence from food and a day or two on water and fruit juices will have any effect.

Try to do these breathing exercises regularly. They can be performed sitting at an office desk or standing by a machine in a factory, or while driving in a car. Sitting in a recognized Yoga pose is best, because in this position the body can be erect and relaxed at the same time. While standing, the limbs which hold the body in position cannot be relaxed.

Naturally Erect
The insistence on a *naturally* erect position during breathing has, as we now know, a scientific basis. Mathias Alexander, who cured thousands of people of tension by making them sit and walk naturally, was a student of Yoga. His theory was that an unnatural relation of the head to the neck is responsible for more afflictions than most people realize: fibrositis, lumbago, fallen arches, flat feet, and even apparently unconnected ailments such as asthma. His assistant, Charles Neill was, in fact, a martyr to asthma before he met Alexander.

"I don't claim to cure people of these ills," Alexander used to explain; "I merely teach them how to use their bodies so that they may cure themselves." Faulty posture, he maintained, is at the root of many diseases.

YOGA AND DIET

The Yogi who has obtained complete control over his body can eat and drink almost anything without adversely affecting his constitution. But he is just the person who has no desire whatever, to do so.

He may even swallow without disaster, poisons in sufficiently large doses to kill a dozen normal men, for constant Yoga practice attunes the system to resisting their corroding effects. Then by means of certain cleansing processes not revealed in any book I know, he can throw them out of his system before they injure the organs. He must, however, take action immediately after imbibing poisons or acids otherwise even he will die, as did Swami Narasingha, who habitually swallowed nitric acid, sulphuric acid, carbolic acid, and potassium cyanide to demonstrate his powers. On a final occasion after eating broken glass and half-inch nails and wsahing the lot down with *aqua regia* (a mixture of nitric and hydrolic acids, so called because it can dissolve the "noble" metals, gold and platinum), he omitted to take the necessary cleansing precautions at once, and expired in agony hours later.

Even in the East, however, not one in hundreds of millions is as adept, and until one attains a complete mastery of the body it is necessary to bring the constituents of the blood to a correct balance and build up resistance to disease.

Eat in Solitude

The first piece of advice that Yoga gives about eating is that one should do so either in silence or in solitude. This is almost impossible and often undesirable in a "civilized" community, and is asking a lot from a gregarious animal. So due allowance must be made for modern conditions. If you eat in the company of others, see that they are kindred spirits and the conversation congenial.

Never Eat When Emotionally Overwrought

Never eat when in the throes of violent or pent-up emotion. Scientists tell us that under such conditions the secretion of digestive juices is inhibited and food remains undigested, leading to intestinal trouble. Some years ago the American medical press reported the case of a man who committed suicide in the presence of his wife, who was nursing a baby. She was so distraught by emotion that chemical changes took place in her milk. When the baby was next fed, it was poisoned and died.

This is, of course, an extreme case but it shows how advanced in thought the yogis were many centuries ago.

The Yoga rule of silence is practised in monasteries where monks, while eating, listen to one of their brothers reciting passages from some uplifting work. This may not appeal to all and there is no reason why pleasant conversation or good music should not accompany well cooked food. The mouth was designed by nature to eat, or talk with; not to do both simultaneously. It is uncivilized to gobble and gabble. The habit of reading at meals, so deplored by Victorians as unmannerly, is a sound one, for it induces a peaceful frame of mind and tends to shelve worries and fears. It may not be sociable; but so much that is sociable is also reprehensible.

Mental Attitude to Food

One's mental attitude to food is more important to health than most of us realize. We wonder why some eat the most nourishing foods, adhere strictly to a wise regimen and yet look reedy and under-nourished, whereas others who eat everything that is supposed to be bad for them and live like rakes appear hale and hearty and happy. More often than not their mental attitude is reponsible.

Exercise Tolerance

Yogis urge one to be tolerant. It is usual for meat eaters to sneer at vegetarians as insipid intellectuals, fussy and finicky; and for vegetarians to look down their noses at carnivora. Both adopt the wrong attitude. According to the yogis it is not merely the food one eats that nourishes but the mental attitude with which both food and companions are approached. Does not Paul say in his Epistle to the Romans (14: 14): "There is nothing unclean in itself, but to him that esteemeth anything to be unclean, *to him it is* unclean".

Yogis are essentially vegetarians. They believe it wrong to kill and unaesthetic to eat meat. But they also say that offending the susceptibilities of others is a heinous social offence. If a vegetarian visits the home of one who is not, and the host's wife in her ignorance places meat before her guest, it is not only his duty to eat it but to praise her skill in preparing the food. If suddenly he should spring upon her the information that he is a vegetarian she will grow upset, emotional turmoil will be stirred up inside her and her harmony will be destroyed. There is such a thing as "guestpitality" as well as hospitality.

Vegetarians in their desire to be strict and pure sometimes overlook the harm and resentment they create in others by their "holier than thou" attitude. So be tolerant of the feeding habits of others. Yoga is not a cult of extremes.

Can You Keep Fit on a Vegetarian Diet?

If you accept the true spirit of Yoga, which is neither to kill nor to eat that which others have killed, you will become a vegetarian; but this is an ideal and difficult to put into practice, especially if you were born into a meat-eating family and have enjoyed flesh foods all your life. For such people vegetarianism becomes merely an ordeal unless backed by conviction and *knowledge*, for knowledge about food is needed if you are to live on a vegetarian diet and keep fit.

The consumption of vegetarian food will not necessarily ensure fitness; among the ranks of vegetarians one finds some of the weediest people on earth, as prone to disease as anyone else, simply because they do not know which foods to eat, or how to balance their diet.

Either yogis had an instinctive knowledge of what was good for them, or their knowlege was born of trial and error over a period of years. Swami Sivananda says: "The right kind of food is most important. Half the illnesses of the nation (India) are due to an ill-balanced diet. There is no mystery about diet. It can be learnt very easily".

This may be true but even in an "advanced" society such as ours, if you visit a doctor the odds are that he will not talk to you about diet but will write a prescription for medicines, pills or drugs. Recently a friend who consulted his doctor because he had high blood pressure and suffered from tension and giddiness, came away from the surgery with three kinds of pills: to reduce blood pressure, prevent giddiness, and tranquillize.

"What did he say about diet?" I asked.

"Nothing. Not a word. The pills will do everything."

"What about salt? Didn't he tell you to cut it out or reduce it?"

"Oh, no – the pills will do everything."

Balance Your Meals

Yogis believe in an all-round diet of fresh vegetables and fruit, which we know provide mineral salts and vitamins; nuts and legumes, which we know are rich in fats and proteins; grain and the by-products of grain, such as flour, and root vegetables, which provide carbohydrates; and milk and milk products, such as butter, cheese and yogurt. Oddly enough, this confirms the most up-to-date scientific thinking about food which lays down that we need carbohydrates, proteins, fats, minerals salts and vitamins for perfect health. They didn't have to worry about vitamin D because India has plenty of sun, or vitamin B_{12} because the mustard oil with which they massage their bodies before basking, is rich in it.

Can One Remain Strong on a Vegetarian Diet?

Before the war there lived a family of amateur

champion wrestlers named Bacon (an odd name for vegetarians!) whose strength and stamina were never questioned by those they defeated. A former lightweight boxing champion of the world, Freddie Welch, was a vegetarian. So was Jim Londos, a Greek, who was heavyweight wrestling champion of the world. Most Hindu wrestlers are vegetarians. Gama, who put the mighty Pole Zbysko on his back in a few seconds and robbed him of the world's heavyweight title, lived on *chappattis* (unleavened wholemeal bread), milk products, nuts, fruit, vegetables, lentils and millet. Healthy vegetarians abound wherever you look. In Britain there is a Vegetarian Cycling Club whose members have broken innumerable endurance records.

The Example of China

Millions in China live on a vegetarian diet because they are too poor to buy meat. Those who live near rivers eat fish, but the soya bean keeps most of them fit. It is richer in protein than any known food and, according to Henry C. Sherman, Mitchill Professor of Chemistry, Columbia University: "Chemical research on the amino-acid constitution of animal proteins and nutritional research with human subjects in balance experiments with laboratory animals over long segments of the life cycle (including the periods of rapid growth) rank the proteins of 'soybeans' and peanuts with animal proteins in chemical nature and nutritional efficiency; and show further that the proteins of our ordinary beans and peas need but little supplementation in order to nourish us equally well".*

*Food Values and Management

Sherman also says: "Tradition has accumulated a strong prejudice which attributes superiority to 'animal protein' and inferiority to the proteins of vegetable foods. This we know from modern research to be an unsound generalization, yet this prejudiced and prejudicial inheritance from a pre-scientific yesterday persists. ..." The relative protein values of some foods are shown below: one ounce of soya bean contains 9.6 grams of protein; mutton 5.97, fish 5.5, chicken 6.74, egg 3.79, wholemeal flour 3.90, and peas 1.85.

Soya can grow wherever wheat and rice flourish and a country like India would go a long way to solving her problems if soya beans were grown instead of rice, or in addition to rice.

Opinions of Eminent Physicians

J. Ellis Barker (not a vegetarian), the famous homoeopath, wrote: "I not only make all my patients vegetarians, but I explain why I do so, and if they hesitate to accept my views, I tell them that milk is liquid beef, that eggs are concentrated chicken, that cheese is beef in another form, etc."

There is no vegetarian food that does not contain some carbohydrate. In *The Bacteriology of Food*, Dr. C. Dukes writes: "Different types of microbes cause different kinds of decomposition in food, divisible roughly into two main varieties: *fermentation* due to the decomposition of carbohydrates, and *putrefaction* due to the decomposition of (flesh) proteins. Where the products of the former are usually harmless, those of the latter are invariably objectionable".

If you have a sound digestion and excrete regularly, you can eat flesh food and keep fit; but if your digestion is bad and you suffer from constipation, the putrefaction of meat will cause auto-intoxication and brings about illness. Pavlov showed by experiments that the liver has to work three times as hard on a meat diet. Every meat-eater should drastically reduce the amount of flesh products he eats after the age of 40.

Stamina and Endurance

In their book *How to Live*, Dr. Fisher and Dr. Fisk say: "Meat eating and a high protein diet, instead of increasing one's endurance, have shown, like alcohol, actually to reduce it." They conducted experiments on 49 subjects, instructors and students at Yale; athletes accustomed to high-protein and full-flesh dietary; athletes accustomed to low-protein and non-flesh dietary; and sedentary workers accustomed to low protein and non-flesh dietary. All the low-protein and non-flesh subjects except one had abstained from flesh foods for periods ranging from four to 20 years. Five had never touched meat. It was found in every test that those who did not eat meat had greater stamina than those that did.

One test isn't much use, so let us turn to the *Report of the United States National Conservation Commission*, Vol. III, page 665, which states: "Comparative experiments on 17 vegetarians and 25 meat eaters in the laboratory of the University of Brussels have shown little difference in strength between the two classes, but a *marked* superiority of the vegetarian in point of endurance".

Sir Herman Weber, the famous physician, who died at 95 in full possession of his faculties, though not a vegetarian, was greatly in favour of reduced consumption of meat with advancing age. In

Prolongation of Life, he writes: "Many years ago I observed on myself that the reduction of the amount of food, especially meat and other flesh food, to half the quantity I had been in the habit of taking, enabled me to do a larger amount of work without the feeling of mental exhaustion, and craving for tea or coffee some hours after a meat meal.

"During my observations on this subject, extending over more than 60 years, I have been able to inquire into the manner of living and other antecedents of over 100 persons living to between 86 and 100 years. Although most of these persons belonged to the well-to-do classes, and were not obliged to restrict themselves, there are not more than six among them who had more or less habitually indulged themselves by eating and drinking largely; many on the contrary, were remarkable for great moderation in both eating and drinking; some lived almost entirely on vegetables and fruit in great quantities, with the addition of milk, cheese, butter and occasionally eggs, and only quite exceptionally took meat, fish and poultry. ...

"I often succeeded in curing eczema, acne, roughness and scaliness of the skin and foetor (foulness) of breath, by total abstinence during months and years from flesh and fish, and the substitution of vegetables, especially green vegetables, milk, cheese and eggs with moderation. Not rarely this diet led also, as already mentioned, to great improvement of the complexion. It is worth mentioning that according to recent researches, the vegetable albumins show greater resistance to poisonous bacteria than animal albumins, and they are probably less prone to auto-intoxication".

It is not my intention to turn people from flesh-eating to vegetarianism. I am not a reformer and don't believe in trying to reform others. One can but produce facts and allow people to make up their own minds. If, however, you've read so far you must have some interest in the subject and have wondered why the yogis advocated vegetarianism.

Does Meat Induce Violent Temper?

I have never advanced this theory, but the yogis say it does! So did Dr. A. Lapthorn Smith in *How To Be Useful and Happy From* 60 *to* 90, which was published in his 91st year. He writes about a patient whose body and arms were covered with bruises from beatings her husband had given her.

"Is your husband a big meat-eater?" asked Lapthorn Smith.

"Yes, three meals a day and at each meal a pound or more of meat."

"Cut down the quantity," he advised; "make it up with other food and say you can't afford so much meat."

After a month her husband beat her less frequently and when his ration was reduced to half a pound of meat a day the beatings ceased altogether! One doubts whether this would be effective with all meat eaters; but it's worth trying.